Sweetie Ladd's

Historic
Fort Worth

Cissy Stewart Lale

SWEETIE LADD'S
HISTORIC FORT WORTH

Paintings by Sweetie Ladd
Text by Cissy Stewart Lale

TCU PRESS · FORT WORTH

Library of Congress Cataloging-in-Publication Data

Lale, Cissy Stewart.
    Sweetie Ladd's historic Fort Worth : paintings by Sweetie Ladd / text by Cissy Stewart Lale.
        p   cm.
    Includes bibliographical references
    ISBN 0-87565-196-8 (cloth : alk. Paper). – ISBN 0-87565-197-6
(pbk. : alk. paper)
        1   Ladd, Sweetie, 1902-1991—Themes, motives. 2. Fort Worth
(Tex.)—In art.   I. Ladd, Sweetie, 1902-1991. II. Title. III. Title: Historic Fort Worth.
ND237.L217L35   1999
759.13—dc21   98-48790
                                                                   CIP

The Sweetie Ladd paintings and lithographs in this book are in the collection of the Fort Worth Public Library.

Publication of this book in Fort Worth's sesquicentennial year was made possible by generous grants from Kay Dickson Farman, the Summerlee Foundation of Dallas, the Fort Worth Public Library, and the Friends of the Fort Worth Public Library. Funds from the Library and the Friends represent donations in memory of the late Irvin S. Farman.

Book, Jacket Design/Margie Adkins Graphic Design

In Memory of Irvin S. Farman

Journalist, Historian, Bookman
Fort Worth is not the same without him.

Contents

Sweetie Ladd was a sophisticated woman who deliberately chose the medium of folk art to preserve Fort Worth history and leavened that history with her own memories, her love of people and her special sense of humor.

Ladd took a light-hearted approach to her art. She once advised a fellow artist studying her folk-art style to "just paint poorly, dear." But she had an historian's dedication to accuracy when it came to painting Fort Worth landmarks. She told a *Fort Worth Star-Telegram* reporter in 1976 that it wasn't unusual for her to wake up in the middle of the night trying to remember whether the interurban did indeed stop in front of the building she was drawing or a block away.

She researched the history of buildings and events at the Fort Worth Public Library and often painted scenes from the library's collection of historic Fort Worth photographs. What makes her work uniquely her own, however, is the people, clothing, animals and details from her memory.

The Fort Worth Public Library owns probably the largest single collection of Sweetie Ladd works; fittingly the Central Library at 300 Taylor Street was built in part on land once occupied by the Ladd Furniture Company where Sweetie Ladd's first artistic endeavor was illustrating furniture store advertisements.

Ladd was not a native of the city she sought to preserve in art. She was born in Bonham, the fifth child of Edgar and Lou Kerr. One of her three sisters insisted that the baby be called Sweetie, "because she is so sweet." She was named Ileta for legal documents, but family and friends always called her Sweetie and few were aware that she had a more formal name. As an artist, she regretted her name. "People think I'm not sophisticated," she told a reporter.

The Kerr family moved to Fort Worth in 1905 when Sweetie's father, rancher and cattleman Edgar Kerr, affiliated with the Cassidy Southwestern Commission Company. The Kerrs were "somewhat well-to-do," the artist once recalled. "We had a nice home on Hemphill, and two horses and a surrey that we sold for an automobile as soon as they were available."

Sweetie Ladd grew up in Fort Worth's cattle heyday, when cattle barons were building homes along Summit Avenue and downtown buildings were not simply buildings but monuments to the builders. As a schoolgirl, Sweetie swam with her friends on Saturdays at the Turkish Baths in the rococo Natatorium Building, followed by ice cream sodas at Booth's Confection. She had dates to see Eddie Cantor and Will Rogers at the Majestic Theater on Monday nights—"the society night." Her parents made a concession to permit her to attend on Mondays, which were school nights, with her special beau, Homer Ladd, five years her senior. "I was kind of grown up," Sweetie recalled.

She remembered dances at Lake Erie during her courtship with Homer Ladd. "We never rode the Interurban because Homer's dad had a Studebaker. We complained that the Studebaker jarred your eye-teeth, so his dad bought a Franklin and we bounced in that." Sweetie graduated from Fort Worth's Central High School and received a degree from Texas Christian University, in English and Spanish, in 1932, after her marriage to Homer Ladd and the birth of their only child, Homer Ladd, Jr.

Although her paintings are classified as folk art, Sweetie Ladd never fit the definition of self-taught artist. She was a sophisticated woman who traveled throughout the United States and Europe. She was a charter member of the Woman's Club of Fort Worth, Fort Worth Garden Club and Woman's Wednesday Club as well as a member of the Lecture Foundation. Both Sweetie and Homer were members of First Presbyterian Church. When she decided to study art at the age of sixty, she joined the art department of the Woman's Club of Fort Worth where her instructors included one of Texas' leading painters, Bror Utter. Later she took workshops taught by artist Frederic Taubes, who recognized her unique talent as a "primitive" artist and urged her to forego additional instruction and simply paint what she remembered. Ladd took his advice. For the rest of her long life, she concentrated on painting. She gave up teaching the nondenominational Rae Reimers Bible Class with its membership of prominent Fort Worth women—a post she held for forty years—to attend a class on perspective at Texas Christian University. She rose at six-thirty each morning to allow herself two hours for painting.

Her first paintings were a series, "Cries of Fort Worth," inspired by Wheatley's "Cries of London," etchings of peddlers in late eighteenth-century London. Her work frequently was compared to that of Grandma Moses who painted primitive views of her New England childhood. A close friend of Ladd's objected to the comparison: "Grandma Moses was a simple person; Sweetie Ladd is not." Sweetie Ladd searched the dictionary and coined her own term for her work: "eclectic primitive."

Although she became an artist late in life, Sweetie Ladd lived to see her work widely acclaimed. Her painting of a 1908 Sunday School picnic at the original Broadway Presbyterian Church was included in the "American Painters in Paris" exhibition in 1976 that was part of the French recognition of the American bicentennial.

In 1982, gallery owner Ron Hall gave Sweetie Ladd a one-person show at his Sundance Gallery in Fort Worth. All of the paintings, watercolors and etchings at that time on permanent loan to the Fort Worth Public Library were included in the show. "It sold out," Hall remembers. "In addition to the interest in local settings, people responded to the affection with which she treated her themes." Dr. Paula Tyler of Austin, who was director of Sundance Gallery at the time, pointed out that "One of the charms of Sweetie's painting is the humor and wit in it." A Sweetie Ladd painting recently reproduced on the cover of the *Southwestern Historical Quarterly* is from the private collection of Paula Tyler and her husband, Dr. Ron C. Tyler.

Sweetie Ladd painted almost to the day of her death on April 26, 1991, at the age of eighty-nine. When her hand shook so that she could no longer master watercolor, she produced hand-colored engravings. Her husband, Homer William Ladd , died in 1978. Their only child, Homer William Ladd Jr., died in 1997 and is buried in Mount Olivet Cemetery beside his parents.

Fort Worth never suffered the conflagrations that destroyed much of Chicago and London, but the south side of the city burned on April 3, 1909, and for a time the entire business district was threatened. The fire finally was brought under control when it reached the open park between the Texas & Pacific Railroad yards and Front Street.

Some 250 homes, a number of small businesses, Broadway Baptist Church, Broadway Presbyterian Church, the Texas & Pacific roundhouse, shops, twenty steam engines and 150 railroad cars were destroyed. The Texas & Pacific depot was saved when a bucket brigade joined with the Fort Worth Fire Department, the North Fort Worth Fire Department and the Dallas Fire Department.

The *Austin American-Statesman* reported "Fort Worth fire greatest ever recorded in that section of the magnificent state." Damages were estimated at $3,500,000. Eight Fort Worth firefighters were injured but only one man, J.J. Newlon, died. The blaze, which burned for more than three hours, apparently was started about 1:00 P.M. by "small boys" smoking cigarettes in the barn of the Fred L. Hackett residence at the corner of Peter Smith Street and Jennings Avenue.

Oil and coal in the Texas & Pacific shops stoked the fire, sending a dark cloud of smoke sweeping through the business district. It was that dark smoke that Sweetie Ladd remembered. Only a child, she managed to slip away from home to watch the fire. Her mother sent an older sister to bring Sweetie home, but the sister remained until a neighbor was sent to bring both girls home. Sweetie Ladd painted all three into the fire scene. Two young boys in the painting probably were Otto and Oscar Monnig whose family-owned department store, Monnig's, is advertised on the billboard at lower right.

Fort Worth's first firefighting unit, made up entirely of volunteers, was formed in 1873 after an editorial campaign by pioneer editor B.B. Paddock in his newspaper, *Fort Worth Democrat*. The volunteers not only contributed their services but bought the city's first firefighting apparatus—a hand-drawn hook-and-ladder which they pulled to Fort Worth from Dallas, the nearest railhead. At the time of the south side fire, Fort Worth had a professional fire department and horse-drawn equipment. The fire horses were highly trained and knew their jobs as well as the firemen. When the fire alarm sounded, stalls opened automatically so the horses could move to posts in front of the wagons, harnesses dropped from the ceiling, and in minutes firemen and firewagons headed for the blaze.

Shortage of water was a problem for firefighters at the south side blaze. They reported their pumpers were "sucking air." Shortly after the fire, Mayor W. D. Daves conceived the plan of building Lake Worth to provide adequate water for the city. Lake Worth was constructed in 1916. In 1910, a year after the great fire, Fort Worth purchased its first two motorized fire trucks.

The Day Ft Worth Burned   April 3, 1909
Sweetie Ladd

Sweetie Ladd is believed to have painted this view of the original Fort Worth Children's Hospital in 1976 for a Christmas card to be sold by the board of the hospital. The board, however, decided on a scene with Santa Claus.

Ida L. Turner, one of Fort Worth's three women postmistresses who served prior to women's suffrage, was waiting for a streetcar one cold day in November 1917 when she noticed a young physician she knew carrying an obviously sick infant. Mrs. Turner asked the doctor why he was on the street with a sick baby. The baby had been abandoned in the doctor's office, and he had been unable to find any institution to care for it.

Mrs. Turner realized that Fort Worth had no infirmary, orphanage or hospital to care for ill infants and young children. She mobilized her friends and the City Federation of Women's Clubs, and by the following March, the twenty-five bed Fort Worth Free Baby Hospital opened at 2400 Winton Terrace West.

The hospital was built in typical Fort Worth fashion. According to the *Fort Worth Star-Telegram*: "The ground, the lumber, the labor, and finally the furnishings for the building were donated. Everything about the hospital is a gift of some citizen or firm in Fort Worth. The children's hospital has been fostered by the City Federation of Women's Clubs and has been furthered by all the woman's organizations in the city, as well as by citizens who are members of no organization. The churches, labor unions and various organizations have been active in the work of completing the hospital."

Dr. K.H. Beall was the first physician, Katherine Van Doren was the first superintendent. Nursing students from St. Joseph's Hospital and the Johnson-Beall Sanitarium assisted them. A two-month old baby brought from West Texas was the first patient. Four years later, the hospital expanded to include thirty beds for infants and fifteen beds for children ages four to fifteen.

In order to provide fresh milk and vegetables for the patients, the hospital kept several milk cows and a large garden. The women continued to support the hospital, not only with donations but by assuming the responsibility of cooking meals for both patients and staff. Although private patients paid for their own hospitalization, no child in need of medical care was turned away because a parent or guardian was unable to pay.

By 1953, Fort Worth Children's Hospital—as the hospital had been named—was described as "woefully inadequate" by its own board of directors. It had no operating room, no isolation ward at a time when polio epidemics swept Texas almost every summer. Mrs. Nenetta Burton Carter and Mrs. A. Renerick (Billie) Clark organized the Jewel Charity Ball to provide funds for children whose families could not pay for their care. By 1998 the annual Jewel Charity Ball had contributed more than $17,759,711 to care for hospitalized children.

The second Fort Worth Children's Hospital building at the corner of Sixth Avenue and Pruitt Street was dedicated in 1961. Fort Worth Children's Hospital merged with Cook Children's Hospital to form Cook Children's Medical Center, which opened its 183-bed hospital at 801 Seventh Avenue in 1989.

Ft. Worth Children's Hospital
1918

Sweetie Ladd
'76

7

Courthouses were more than the visible seats of county government on the Texas frontier. They were both the social gathering places and the market centers of the county. Fort Worth won the county seat designation in 1856 in a bitter election with Birdville which had been named county seat in 1850. Some authorities say Fort Worth won the election by thirteen votes; others say the margin was a little as three votes. Birdville citizens claimed that "Fort Worth voted every man as far west as the Rio Grande."

The following year, Captain Ephraim Merrell Daggett, known as the father of Fort Worth, sent wagons and ox carts to Cherokee County to buy lumber to build a small, three-room courthouse west of the present Tarrant County Courthouse. The building was designed with a wide hall running through the center, and the town's inebriates as well as stray hogs frequently spent nights in the hall. Inspired by continual agitation of Birdville for another county seat election, forty-one Fort Worth citizens subscribed $2,700 to build a stone-and-brick courthouse in 1859, but before the foundation was laid, the Texas Legislature called an election for "a permanent county seat."

Fort Worth won the designation on April 28, 1860; on March 2, 1861, Texas seceded from the Union and two days later joined the Confederate States of America. Building was discontinued during the Civil War and the first stone courthouse was not completed until the early 1870s. It burned in 1876. The courthouse in Sweetie Ladd's painting was built in 1876-1877 and was razed in 1894 to make way for the present courthouse.

The wagons loaded with cotton probably came from the Boaz and Battle cotton yard which operated on the courthouse square in the 1870s and 1880s. Market days were regular events on the courthouse square and on those occasions, farm wagons jammed the square.

The year 1876 defined the future of Fort Worth. Texas & Pacific's Engine #20 pulled into Fort Worth on July 19 on tracks laid by residents working around the clock because the state's land grant agreement with the railroad was to be voided if the railroad did not reach Fort Worth before the Texas Legislature adjourned. The first natural gas plant opened, providing gas lighting; the first telegraph line was strung to Dallas, and on Christmas day, the first mule-drawn streetcar transported passengers from the courthouse to the T&P Station. The streetcar frequently jumped the tracks and passengers were called upon to get out and lift the car back onto the tracks. Some passengers complained they worked harder than the mules. During its first year of operation, the two mule-drawn streetcars made 160 trips per day carrying an average of 440 passengers for a daily profit of $22.

Second Tarrant County Court House
1876 – 1894
First Street car (1876) Mule drawn

Sweetie Ladd
73

9

The Spring Palace was called "the pride and glory of Texas." Built at a cost of $100,000, the palace was constructed in the shape of a St. Andrew's cross with a massive 150-foot dome, "surpassed in size only by the nation's Capitol." Every inch of the 225 x 375 foot structure, except the floors, was covered with the products of Texas arranged to depict typical state scenes. Fort Worth women spent long hours decorating the interior with wheat, corn stalks, cactus, rye, moss, cotton—and even Johnson grass. Roofs of the twelve Moorish towers were covered with shelled corn and oats, and strings of popcorn and peas curtained the windows. Special excursion trains came from as far away as Boston to tour the palace.

The palace opened May 10, 1889. In spite of a large attendance, however, the palace recorded a $23,000 deficit in its first year of operation. A hundred feet of space was added to each wing for the second season, and cities and counties from all over the state were assigned space. Some of these other areas are apparent in Sweetie Ladd's painting of the Spring Palace. Fort Worth women were organized into ten groups, and each group worked eight to ten hours a day for more than a hundred days to decorate the building. In its second season, the Spring Palace was a financial success.

On May 30, 1890, a dress ball was scheduled. More than a thousand people came from Dallas for the occasion. An estimated 7,000 people were in the building, most of them in the 16,000-foot ballroom, when the structure was swept by fire. The decorations of dry moss, grass and straw instantly burst into flames. In four minutes the building was a mass of flame, and in eleven minutes it fell to the ground. Fire spread so rapidly that firemen stationed in various parts of the building, holding hoses connected to fire hydrants, did not have time to turn on the water.

Officials directed visitors to the sixteen exits in the building. Although some thirty people were injured, most of them women wearing low-necked, short sleeved dresses that exposed them to falling cinders, only Al Hayne, the hero of the disaster, died. Hayne made several trips into the burning building, dropping children and women from second-story windows into the arms of men below. With his clothing ablaze, he leaped from the window with a woman in his arms. The woman survived but Hayne died three hours later. A monument was erected in his memory at the site of the palace, just south of the intersection of Lancaster and Main streets.

Fort Worth was consoled by the reaction of newspapers and magazines throughout the country. *Frank Leslie's Illustrated Newspaper* published one of the most prophetic articles: "Fort Worth is one of the most enterprising cities in Texas, and it is safe to say that even the destruction of its magnificent Spring Palace, which has attracted visitors from every section of the Union, will not dampen the ardor of its citizens nor lessen the magnificent prosperity which it rightfully enjoys."

Fort Worth's first big hotel was the Worth Hotel, built in 1894 by John Scharbauer and W. C. Stonestreet at Seventh and Main streets. The hotel endured until the 1920s when the Citizens Hotel Company headed by William Monnig raised $2 million by public subscription, bought and razed the Worth, and replaced it with the Texas Hotel which opened in 1921 at Eighth and Main. The renovated Texas Hotel is the present Radisson Plaza Hotel Fort Worth.

Hotels are a barometer for a city's growth. Captain E. M. Daggett opened Fort Worth's first hotel in the old army stable vacated by the horses of Major Ripley Arnold and his Dragoons. Quanah Parker, last chief of the Comanches, narrowly escaped death at the El Paso Hotel in 1878 when he extinguished the flame in the gas light without turning off the jet. Fortunately, his friend, Colonel E. L. Elbert of Quanah, Hardeman County, sensed the escaping gas and rescued Quanah.

One of the most glamorous hotels in Fort Worth history was the Metropolitan, a three-story brick building erected in 1898 at Ninth and Main. The Metropolitan offered rooms with electricity, steam heat, and artesian baths for fifty cents to $1 a day. There was both a hack stand and a streetcar line in front of the hotel. A caller from the T&P Station regularly came to the hotel to announce departure and arrival of trains at the nearby station.

The Metropolitan was famous as the scene of two sensational murders. Beal Sneed, an Amarillo cattleman, shot Capt. A.G. Boyce, manager of the Capitol Ranch near Amarillo, as he sat reading a newspaper in the hotel lobby. Sneed's wife had run away with Boyce's son, Al Boyce, Jr. Twenty years later, in 1913, Whitmore Stonewell Phillips shot E.L. Churchill in the lobby over the affections of a hotel stenographer, Sally Moore.

When the Citizens Hotel Corporation organized to raise funds to build the Hotel Texas, it raised $1,200,000 for the new hotel at a dinner held in the Metropolitan. The Metropolitan was sold to the Milner Hotel chain in 1938 and was razed in 1959 for a parking lot. President John F. Kennedy made his last speech on that lot the morning of November 22, 1963. He was assassinated later that day in Dallas.

Most of the first class hotels in Fort Worth prior to the 1930s were multi-story with much of the first floor dedicated to stores totally unrelated to the hotel. August's clothing store occupied the prime corner location at the Worth Hotel. Many hotel guests were permanent residents. Winfield Scott resided at the Worth Hotel for nine months while Thistle Hill was being remodeled to the taste of his wife, Elizabeth Scott. Mrs. Scott and their young son, Winfield Scott Jr., commuted to Fort Worth from their home in St. Louis as the remodeling progressed. Winfield Scott died before he could move into his mansion—still a resident of the Worth Hotel.

Jesse Jones of Houston opened a second Worth Hotel in 1927 at Seventh and Taylor streets. That eighteen-story hotel was imploded October 29, 1972, to make way for a fourteen-story addition to the Fort Worth Club building and a parking garage.

Worth Hotel (BUILT 1894)
Sweetie Ladd 1975

13

The turreted red sandstone post office at corner of Jennings Avenue and Eleventh Street was something of a Fort Worth triumph when it opened in 1896. It took seven years and nine acts of Congress to get the building funded. When the bill to fund the project first was introduced on March 2, 1889, Congress was in a stingy mood and appropriated only $75,000 to purchase a site and construct the building. The next year, the appropriation was raised to $175,000, and four years later it was raised again to $215,000, but it took three other appropriations for the building and three additional bills for additions and improvements.

The building was the first in Fort Worth designed as a post office but it also housed the city's first federal district court, the weather bureau and other federal offices. The first postmaster in the new post office building was Ida L. Turner, the third woman to hold that office in Fort Worth. Her predecessors were Mrs. Dorcas Williams, appointed by President Andrew Johnson in 1886, and Mrs. Belle M. Burchill who inaugurated home delivery of mail in 1884. All three women served before women were given the right to vote by the 19th Amendment in 1920. Turner and her staff complained bitterly about the smell of fresh paint when they moved in. Most Fort Worth residents were awed by the new post office. Before it opened, mail was delivered from the first floor of the old Board of Trade building at Seventh and Houston streets. Customers told reporters what they liked best about the new post office was that they had ample room to line up for their mail on Sundays.

In addition to its four turrets, the building's roof boasted a weather bureau observation deck reached by a kind of ship's ladder from the fourth floor. The post office interior was equipped with brass light fixtures designed for both gas and electricity, marble sinks and wash basins, a bathtub with a wooden rail around the top (nobody knows why it was there), solid oak staircases with hand-carved posts, windows made of quarter-inch thick glass, curved to fit the bay windows, and an open-sided elevator. A well in the basement supplied water. There were copper ornaments on the slate roof and elaborate drain spouts carved in the shape of gargoyles, so unique they were given to the Fort Worth Art Association.

In 1937, the city of Fort Worth bought the structure from the federal government for $56,120. Corporation courts, the police warrant division and traffic violation bureau were housed in the building until 1963, when the City Council voted to raze the building to make way for a parking lot. In spite of a protest led by the Tarrant County Historical Society, Mrs. Will F. Collins, Mrs. E. P. Van Zandt and Mrs. Kenneth Garrett, the historic building was demolished in November 1963. In Sweetie Ladd's painting, the wagon at lower right has a Fakes & Co. sign. Fakes was a leading furniture store—and a competitor of the Ladd Furniture Co.

JESUS
SAVES

FAKES & CO
FURNITURE

Federal Building (1896)
(Post Office)(Weather Station)

Ladd '75

15

The Flower Parade and Festival featured flower-bedecked buggies filled with young women wearing fluttering white dresses and flowered hats. The buggies proceeding down Main Street toward the Texas & Pacific Railroad Station in May 1900 provided a sure sign that frontier Fort Worth was adopting refinement.

Three years earlier Captain B.B. Paddock had observed: "Refinement follows wealth according to the law of cause and effect, and social pleasures increase and multiply as refinement ploughs [sic] its way into rugged western life. This has been noticeable in the social status of Fort Worth during the last three years. At the beginning of that period but little attention has been paid to the development or cultivation of social relations among the people.

"The previous seven years in the history of the city has [sic] been spent with everybody in pursuit of money. Many had scarcely expected to make Fort Worth a permanent home, and their minds occasionally went back to scenes of other days in other states. The border roughness was exhilarating in a business view but depressing in its social aspects.

"But by the year 1883, with its era of public improvement, caused a revolution in social affairs. Homes were improved. The city began to have a finished appearance. Shrubbery and shade trees were cultivated. Men of wealth built costly residences. Sidewalks sprang into existence in all parts of the city.

"The churches increased in numbers. Their congregations swelled and the social garden budded and blossomed in proportion to the development of business enterprises. The roughness of frontier life was passing away. The city prospered. Everybody prospered, and life in Fort Worth commenced to adorn itself with comforts and delicacies."

They also adopted the pursuit of culture and good works.

Mrs. John W. Swayne was introduced to the Woman's Club movement during a trip to New York City and, on February 11, 1889, soon after her return to Fort Worth, she invited friends for tea at her home, 503 East First Street. At the tea, she proposed the formation of a club "for the purpose of promoting culture, entertainment and social growth among married ladies of Fort Worth." Records state that Mrs. Swayne wore a pink cashmere tea gown with a train and so eloquently did she speak that the Woman's Wednesday Club was organized that afternoon. The Woman's Wednesday Club, still active more than a hundred years later, was one of the founding groups of the Woman's Club of Fort Worth, organized in 1923. Sweetie Ladd was a member and past president of the Woman's Wednesday Club.

Ladd found it difficult to paint horses—a difficulty that is obvious in her painting, *Fiesta Parade* (1900). In a 1976 interview, the artist told a reporter that a woman had recently examined an array of Sweetie Ladd paintings and remarked, "Well, here, Sweetie, this is your best horse."

16

Fiesta Parade 1900 Ft. Worth, Texas
Sweetie Ladd

The Texas & Pacific Railway depot burned at 2:55 P.M. Saturday, Dec. 17, 1904—the time was recorded on the depot clock. It was among the most spectacular Fort Worth fires, recorded by historic photographs and several paintings. The depot, as all railroad stations were known at the time, opened on January 1, 1900. Its castle-like architecture in red brick with a clock tower marked the south end of the Fort Worth business district, and with the Tarrant County Courthouse at the opposite end of Main Street formed "book ends" for the city. The depot served nearly four railroads into Fort Worth with the exception of the Gulf, Colorado and Santa Fe which opened its own distinctive white-trimmed red brick station at 1501 Jones St. on March 1, 1900, only two months after the T&P Station opened.

Fort Worth was promoted as a rail center "with the only entrance into the great wheat and grain producing country known as the Panhandle or Northwest Texas, making Fort Worth a great shipping and distributing point for all of Texas, New Mexico, old Mexico and Southeastern states."

By 1900, Fort Worth was served by eight "grand trunk" railroads—Texas & Pacific, Gulf, Colorado and Santa Fe, Missouri-Kansas-Texas, Fort Worth and Denver, Rock Island, St. Louis and Southwestern, and Fort Worth and Rio Grande. More than 100,000 visitors arrived annually on those railroads and brought with them some 30,000 pieces of baggage—more than any other depot in the state.

The significance of the railroads to Fort Worth can be judged by population statistics. In 1872, before the city had a railroad connection, Fort Worth had a population of 1500 people at a generous estimate. After the arrival of the first T&P train on July 19, 1876, Fort Worth boomed. Six months later, an estimated 1,000 people lived in tents because no housing was available. During the next decade, the population increased to 23,076 people.

The T&P depot was rebuilt after the 1904 fire and remained a Fort Worth landmark until it was razed in 1931 and replaced by the art deco Texas & Pacific Passenger Terminal designed by Herman Paul Koeppe, chief designer for Wyatt C. Hedrick, and Preston M. Geren. Construction of the new terminal during the height of the Depression helped blunt the devastating economic effect of the period in Fort Worth.

By the 1930s, the T&P terminal served four railroad lines, Texas & Pacific, Fort Worth & Denver, International-Great Northern and the Missouri-Kansas-Texas. The railroad industry employed some 5,500 men and women in Fort Worth and boasted a $7 million annual payroll in the 1930s. The building operated as a passenger terminal until March 22, 1967, when the last train, the Texas & Pacific Eagle, pulled into the station from El Paso.

Ft.Worth's T.&P. Depot
at the turn of the century
Ladd '75

Sweetie Ladd remembered The Natatorium. It was the place she and girl friends went swimming on Saturday afternoons. The Nat, as it was known, had a fifty by ninety-foot swimming pool filled with water from artesian springs. The Nat also offered Turkish baths (the bather passes through a series of steam rooms of increasing temperature and then receives a rubdown, massage and cold shower) and Russian baths (vapor baths consisting of prolonged exposure of the body to steam followed by washings, friction, and a cold plunge).

In an 1893 booklet titled "The Future Metropolis of Texas," Sue Greenleaf wrote: "the four-story Natatorium building cost $150,000 to build. It is fitted with elegant marble bath, swimming pool and Turkish bath facilities. . . . The Natatorium is a private enterprise of which citizens of Fort Worth are justly proud. "

The four-story building at the corner of East Third and Commerce (called Rusk Street in 1900) was a social center with rooms for private parties and clubs as well as a hotel "for gentlemen only." Its rooms were equipped with steam heat, electric lights and "all modern conveniences." In an era when the customary Saturday night bath commonly took place in the kitchen with a large wash tub filled with water heated in a kettle on the kitchen stove, the Natatorium offered ultimate luxury. The facility was first owned and operated by a company composed of W.B. Capps, president; O.B. Canty; vice-president; C. Crane, secretary; and J. E. Johnson, manager. Later, it was sold to Traders Investment Company. James M. Fall was manager.

Baths were a part of Fort Worth history. Trail drivers herding cattle up the Chisholm Trail looked forward to the luxury of a hot bath in Fort Worth as much as other pleasures the city offered. Every major barbershop offered a hot bath along with a shave and a hair cut. The better establishments also provided manicures and pedicures and shoe or boot shines, all for men only, of course.

According to Greenleaf, Fort Worth had thirteen artesian wells with a capacity of 3,200,000 gallons daily in 1893. Artesian wells are made by boring into the earth; when the water table is reached, water flows up like a fountain. Water from these wells was invariably "soft," easily lathered homemade lye soap, and left the skin feeling velvety.

Progress, competition from new hotels, and establishment of country clubs and the Fort Worth Club eventually dimmed the glamour of the Natatorium. The building was torn down to make room for a parking lot.

NATATORIUM — "The Nat"
Turkish Baths — Pool — Rooms
3rd St. at Rusk — Early 1900's
Sweetie Ladd '78

21

First Ward School—Fort Worth's first elementary school building—opened in 1900 at the corner of Second and Crump streets. Education had been available for Fort Worth citizens who could pay to send their children to school since 1853 when John Peter Smith, a twenty-two-year-old graduate of Bethany College in Virginia, opened a private school in a building abandoned earlier that year by the army.

Smith was a major proponent of free public schools, although many Fort Worth citizens opposed a tax-supported school system. Smith, Dr. Carroll M. Peak, and Major K.M. Van Zandt called for an election on the question in 1877, and voters endorsed public schools in a light voter turnout, eighty-five to five. Opponents uncovered a law specifying that two-thirds of property owners must have voted in any election to establish a school system. Smith, Van Zandt, Peak and others insisted on a second election, and Fort Worth again voted for public schools. But opponents of schools obtained a ruling from the Texas attorney general that municipal funds could not be diverted to school purposes. A third time, the pro-school element took the question to the polls. The vote was 425 to forty-five in favor of schools. But the question was not settled. Opposition forces claimed that Fort Worth did not have the population of 10,000 required for any municipality to operate a school system.

A census was required. The city council was ready to give up on public schools, but Smith and Van Zandt donated the $300 to pay for the census, and B.B. Paddock supervised the count. Fort Worth's population totaled 11,136, and free public schools were assured. Alexander Hogg of Marshall was named superintendent. The prevailing attitude in the 1880s was that girls needed little or no education, but Hogg insisted that girls needed as good an education as their brothers, and Fort Worth public schools were coed from the start.

Sweetie Ladd's picture of First Ward School shows boys and girls during recess at the school. The boys in the center of the picture play mumbletypeg with two-bladed pocketknives, commonly called jack-knives. Boys were permitted to carry knives, because a knife was considered a standard part of a boy's equipment. Mumbletypeg consisted of a series of maneuvers concluding with sticking the knife blade in the ground. Losers were required to remove a stick driven in the ground with their teeth—getting a mouthful of dirt in the process. Boys at the lower left play marbles. Girls concentrate on jacks and jump ropes.

Tolling of a bell in the school building tower marked recess, lunchtime, and the beginning and ending of the school day. That historic bell, cast in London in 1782, was brought to Fort Worth originally by Lawrence Steele and used as a dinner bell in the hotel Steele bought from Captain E. M. Daggett. Fort Worth Masonic Lodge #148 preserves the bell in the Masonic Temple. It is believed to be the oldest bell in Fort Worth.

23

This sidewalk art show in front of the Carnegie Library is an appropriate juxtaposition reflecting the library's dual cultural heritage. The Fort Worth Public Library Association was founded in 1892 by women of the city to establish "a public library and art gallery." For six years, they conducted teas, cakewalks, dinners and dances, raising a total of $12,000 for the library. When Mrs. D.B. Keeler decided to ask every man in Fort Worth to donate the price of a good cigar to the library, she even wrote to business tycoon Andrew Carnegie asking him to contribute the price of a cigar. Carnegie, the great benefactor of libraries throughout the country, responded with a $50,000 donation. Fort Worth's library was assured.

The library's opening in October 1901 marked the end of Fort Worth's six-shooter culture and the beginning of its appreciation of art. The Fort Worth Art Association established the Fort Worth Museum of Art on the library's second floor in 1910, making its successor, the Fort Worth Museum of Modern Art, the oldest art museum in Texas.

In 1925, the Fort Worth Art Association purchased Thomas Eakins' painting *The Swimming Hole*, which has been reproduced on a U.S. stamp as an outstanding example of American painting. The Amon Carter Museum purchased the Eakins painting for $10 million in 1990. It remains on view "in perpetuity" as a reminder of the city's distinguished cultural history.

Fort Worth was justifiably proud of its brick Carnegie Library at the intersection of Ninth and Throckmorton streets. Teddy Roosevelt, the first president of the United States to visit Fort Worth, arrived at the T&P Station on April 8, 1905, where he was greeted by a crowd of more than 20,000 persons. Roosevelt made a single stop in Fort Worth: he planted an elm tree on the library grounds before leaving on a wolf hunt with Fort Worth ranchers Burk Burnett and W. T. Waggoner.

During the Depression, the Carnegie Library obtained Public Works Administration funds for a new library building, and in spite of considerable controversy, the original building was razed and a new library built on the same site. That building stood vacant when the Central Fort Worth Public Library moved to its present location at 300 Taylor Street and was razed in 1990. Portions of the land on which the library is built once were occupied by the Ladd Furniture Company, owned by Sweetie Ladd's husband, Homer Ladd, and his family.

Tragically, Fort Worth's Carnegie Library was restricted to "whites only" until the U.S. Supreme Court outlawed segregation in 1955.

The Fort Worth Public Library now includes regional libraries, branch libraries and satellite libraries in the Carville and Butler Place housing projects. It is fully computerized and offers interlibrary loan, books on tape, a foreign language collection, an audiovisual collection and public meeting rooms. Its genealogy and local history collection is one of the best in the Southwest. The Sweetie Ladd collection reproduced in this book is part of the library's permanent collection.

CARNEGIE LIBRARY (1901)
Sidewalk Art Show

Sweetie Ladd '75

If there were a single characteristic type of informal recreational architecture in the United States in the early 1900s, it was the pavilion, defined in the dictionary as a "temporary, ornamental and often open shelter used at parks or fairs for amusement or shelter." Of the several such structures in or near Fort Worth, one of the most elaborate was at Lake Erie in Handley, seven miles east of Fort Worth.

Sweetie Ladd painted two scenes of the Lake Erie Pavilion, obviously one of her favorites. The pavilion and the lake were symbolic of a unique method of surface transportation that flourished in that era: the interurban. Cars carrrying several passengers were powered by electricity fed by overhead electric wires. To supply electricity, the interurban companies built power plants which required large amounts of water as a cooling source. Those water sources became a series of lakes, and eventually amusement parks and pavilions were built around those lakes, increasing interurban ridership. By 1900, some two thousand amusement parks had been built in the United States by interurban and streetcar companies. "Pollution" had not yet entered the American vocabulary, so no one thought it strange to be boating, fishing, picnicking and dancing adjacent to a power plant.

The first streetcar line in Fort Worth was the Fort Worth Street Railway Company. As the residential area of the city grew, additional companies were franchised by the city council. The Prairie City Railway Company operated on West Seventh Street, across the Texas & Pacific reservation and on Hemphill Street in the burgeoning south side beginning in 1881. The next company, the Rosedale Street Railway Company, operated from the railroad hospital south of the city along Main Street to the driving park north of town. By 1889, horse- and mule-drawn cars began to be replaced by electrified cars, but the improvement brought small comfort to passengers. Because of inadequate insulation of the cars, passengers often received electrical shocks.

There was no heat in the streetcars until 1909. Motormen standing on open platforms sweltered in the summer and froze in the winter. The Northern Texas Traction Company absorbed the streetcar companies by 1901, the year the Texas Legislature authorized that company to extend rail service to Dallas. One year later, the interurban was running between Fort Worth and Dallas. According to one report, the Crimson Limited Express reached speeds of ninety miles an hour on its run between the two cities, but because passengers could flag and board the train at almost any point, delays were frequent.

Interurban traffic began to decline when roads between Fort Worth and Dallas were paved in the 1930s. The last interurban completed its run on Christmas Eve, 1934, and Texas Electric Service Company moved into the Lake Erie power plant. Demands for electricity in the Fort Worth area brought about an expanded power plant. Lake Erie became part of Lake Arlington, a new water source for the power plant, in 1957.

Lake Erie-Handley Park
Texas Electric Co.
Fort Worth, Texas

Sweetie Ladd
'75

27

Industrial development made and unmade villages and cities in Texas in the early part of the twentieth century. Handley, a village seven miles east of Fort Worth which eventually was absorbed by the larger city, was established in 1884 by the Texas & Pacific Railway. It was named for Major J.M. Handley, a Civil War veteran who owned a plantation east of the community. The village had exactly twelve houses and eighty residents.

Handley began to grow in 1901 when the Fort Worth-Dallas Interurban power plant was opened by the Northern Texas Traction Company. Lake Erie, which supplied water for the power plant's cooling system soon was converted into a park with a two-story auditorium extending over the lake. The interurban brought passengers to the lake in cars often decorated with banners reading "Lake Erie Tonight." Lake Erie closed in the 1930s when the automobile brought about the decline of interurban traffic. Eventually, Texas Electric Service Company took over the power plant.

Handley remained a small village until after World War II. It had one of the last crank-style telephone systems in North Texas, a system that required not only turning a crank to get the attention of a telephone operator but monitoring telephone conversations by the operator to determine when calls were completed. "Modern" telephone equipment replaced the cranks in 1947.

Fort Worth annexed Handley in 1946. Population in the area continued to grow and the demand for electric power increased proportionally. In the 1950s, Texas Electric Service Company installed a 66,000 kilowatt generator—the largest generator in Texas—at the Handley plant. At the same time, Lake Erie was expanded and became part of Lake Arlington. When Lake Arlington was completed in 1957, engineers projected it would take at least four years to fill the lake. Typically perverse North Texas weather provided record rainfall and filled the lake to capacity in twenty-seven days. During the summer of 1998 a prolonged drought and record high temperatures reduced the level of Lake Arlington to dangerous lows, threatening the output of the power plant. Rain eventually prevented a shutdown.

Handley lost its railroad station in 1949. Tom E. Griswold, superintendent of the eastern division of the T & P Railway, testified the Handley station was no longer used for passenger service, and freight at the station had dropped from 202 carloads in 1947 to eighty-four carloads in the first eleven months of 1948. Deserted by both the interurban and the railroad, Handley was swallowed up by Fort Worth.

In the good old summer Time
Lake Erie - Handley Park.
Fort Worth, Texas. 1918

Sweetie Ladd
'75

LAKE ERIE TONIGHT

LAKE ERIE

Lake Como Pavilion was built to attract Arlington Heights streetcar passengers after Lake Como was built as a source of cooling water for the streetcar. It also was part of the promotion by developers of the Arlington Heights addition, when the addition was primarily open pasture. Motormen on the night-line of that particular streetcar route frequently reported hearing wolves howl as their cars bounced across the prairie.

Arlington Heights has been described as a speculator's dream. In 1889 or early 1890, globe-trotting promoter H. B. Chamberlain bought some 2,000 acres from Tom Hurley, a Chicago financier who built Fort Worth's first tall building, the eight-story Hurley Building, and Robert McCart. Chamberlain was a wealthy Denver real-estate man who was president of the world YMCA.

Chamberlain's major contributions to the development of Arlington Heights were Lake Como and Ye Arlington Inn. The inn was described as "the finest hotel in the South, reached by a grand boulevard three and a half miles long and 125 feet wide, macadamized throughout. It has an artificial lake [Lake Como] covering more than forty acres; it has its own waterworks, electric light plant and electric street railway."

The glittering future Chamberlain promoted failed to develop for more than a decade. Ye Arlington Inn burned in 1894. Chamberlain was killed riding a bicycle in a London fog. Fort Worth residents continued to build fine homes on the South Side, ignoring Arlington Heights. One disillusioned investor traded his lot for a set of tires; another traded for a typewriter. Although Lake Como and its elaborate pavilion and amusement park continued to draw patrons, the Arlington Heights addition attracted few homebuilders.

Arlington Heights remained dormant until World War I. When the United States was drawn into the conflict in 1917, Fort Worth leaders made 2,000 acres west of the city, including the Arlington Heights area, available for a military installation that came to be known as Camp Bowie. More than 100,000 doughboys, including the Texas 36th Division, trained at Camp Bowie. When World War I ended and Camp Bowie was closed, the Arlington Heights addition was left with a network of utilities and paved roads.

The demand for homes that finally changed Arlington Heights into the residential area Chamberlain had predicted came in 1917. W.K. Gordon, superintendent of the Texas and Pacific Coal Company coal mine at Thurber, Texas, drilled for oil on a 30,000-acre lease in Eastland County, near Ranger, a hundred miles west of Fort Worth. One October afternoon, oil shot two-thirds the way up the derrick, and the oil boom began. Fort Worth became a concentration point for oil operators.

Lake Como and its elaborate pavilion remained an entertainment mecca for Fort Worth residents until streetcars, the original force behind the pavilion, acknowledged declining revenue and went out of business in the 1930s. Lake Como became a city park managed by the Fort Worth Parks & Community Services Department. By the 1990s, Lake Como Park had a shelter and a pier—but no boardwalk.

Trolleys may come back to Fort Worth. On December 15, 1998, the Fort Worth City Council approved research on building a nine-mile fixed-rail trolley system to connect the city's downtown, historical and cultural districts.

Pavilion, Lake Como (1903-12)
Fort Worth, Texas

Sweetie Ladd
'75

31

When Sweetie Ladd painted Thistle Hill in 1974, the mansion was threatened with demolition. Built for Electra Waggoner and her bridegroom, A.B. Wharton, Jr., in 1903 and remodeled by its second owners, Elizabeth and Winfield Scott, the mansion was the Girls Service League home for underprivileged girls from 1940 until 1968. The Scott House, as it was known, had been designated by a Junior League Survey as one of twelve sites in Fort Worth worthy of preservation, but it was not until September 1974 that a group of concerned citizens met to discuss saving the mansion. Encouraged by small donations, mostly $10 each, the group organized as Save-the-Scott Home (now Texas Heritage, Inc.) and in 1975 leased the mansion for $1000 a month. Members began mopping the pigeon droppings off the floors.

Financial aid came from the Texas Historical Commission and the Community Development program of HUD, the Fort Worth Board of Realtors, the *Fort Worth Star-Telegram*, the auxiliary to St. Demetrios Greek Orthodox Church, the Boy Scouts, numerous small Fort Worth organizations and little old ladies in tennis shoes who remembered driving by the grandest house they could imagine. Ultimately, the ordinary citizens of Fort Worth preserved the mansion that represented the fabulously wealthy cattle barons.

The mansion's name, Thistle Hill, was taken from a plaque over one of the house's fireplaces. The plaque was etched with the word "Rubusmont"—a French or Latin term meaning "Thorn Mountain." For the first ten years, restoration efforts concentrated on the structure of the house. The green tile roof, the foundation, plumbing and wiring were repaired or replaced, and the house was air-conditioned. The grand staircase was repaired, but the ceilings were cracked, the walls streaked and dirty and the scant furnishings inappropriate. In the mid-seventies, architectural students from the University of Texas at Arlington completed a Historic American Building Survey of the building; it was followed in 1982 by a master plan drawn up by the Austin architectural firm of Bell, Klein and Hoffman. Frank Welch, an historic paint consultant, uncovered unusual wall treatments in the library and the upstairs hall, and Michael Berry, curator of interiors for the National Trust for Historic Preservation, furnished a room-by-room plan for the mansion's interior, suggesting furnishings resembling those ordered by Mrs. Scott in 1912. The detailed plans for restoration specified plants and trees on the grounds, including a lowly Chinaberry tree, now labeled a trash tree but considered a perfect shade tree in 1912. Gifts to Thistle Hill gradually furnished the interior in a manner that would have been pleasing to both Electra Waggoner Wharton and Elizabeth Scott.

By the 1990s, some 25,000 people toured the restored mansion each year, guided by trained volunteer docents. Thistle Hill is the site of countless weddings, receptions and parties. As a visible reminder of the city's cattle-baron legacy, Thistle Hill has inspired restoration of other historic structures and homes in Fort Worth and thus established a legacy of its own.

Thistle Hill (1904)
Sweetie Lill
'74

33

In her painting of the Junior Woman's Club, Sweetie Ladd returns the building at 1326 Pennsylvania Avenue to 1905 when it was the home of the J. F. Moore family. In the 1990s, the carefully restored and maintained building has much the same appearance it did shortly after it was built but its setting has changed drastically. The building is across Pennsylvania Avenue from Harris Hospital, and four lanes of automobile traffic have replaced the horse-drawn wagons in the painting. The 700 members of the Junior Woman's Club who presently use the building are young but almost never play hopscotch on the sidewalk. The horse-drawn wagon in the left foreground is from Stripling's, a major downtown Fort Worth department store. Stripling's had a Christmas-theme window with moving figures every holiday. Along with the toy store at Leonard Brothers and the "real" Santa Claus who sat in a sleigh outside Mrs. Baird's Bakery and talked with children, Stripling's and its window meant Christmas for generations of Fort Worth area children.

The Junior Woman's Club building officially is Margaret Meacham Hall, at the west end of the block-long complex of the historic Woman's Club of Fort Worth. Other buildings include Florence Shuman Hall, William G. Newby Memorial Building, Anna Shelton Hall, Waples Hall, Ida Saunders Hall, and Bewley Hall. Sweetie Ladd was a member of the Woman's Club, its Art Department and Woman's Wednesday Club.

Architectural historians describe Margaret Meacham Hall as eclectic in design, with elements of Queen Anne, Mission Revival and Prairie architecture. Its most prominent features are an oriel turret and the stone terrace that wraps around the front of the house. L. B. Weinman designed the house. The building was designated a Recorded Texas Historic Landmark in 1967, and the entire Woman's Club complex received a Texas Historical Commission marker in 1976.

By the 1920s, neither such large mansions and nor the South Side area were considered fashionable. The house became a residence for nurses in 1920 and was known as the Baptist Hospital. Later, it was the Robertson-Mueller-Harper Funeral Home. In 1953, it was purchased by the Woman's Club as headquarters for the Junior Woman's Club and named for Mrs. H. C. Meacham – Margaret Meacham, a charter member of the Woman's Club and the mother-in-law of Fort Worth civic leader Amon G. Carter. Mrs. Meacham had been a member of the Woman's Club committee that organized the Junior Woman's Club in 1926.

The first building in the Woman's Club complex was the William G. Newby Memorial Building, given by Mrs. Newby in 1923 to the newly formed Woman's Club of Fort Worth. G. Palmer Graves designed the two-story brick structure, and Joe Lollar built it in 1910-1911 as a residence of Heinrich Frerichs, a buyer for German cotton interests. Frerichs, suspected of being a high-ranking espionage officer in the German army, fled the United States with his family in 1914, leaving furniture, children's toys and personal possessions in the house. Some of the Frerichs' original furnishings and a few pieces of china remained when Mrs. Newby purchased the home and still are used by the Woman's Club.

J.E. Moore Home - Built 1905
(Junior Woman's Club)
Sweetiedadd '74

The dictionary definition of vaudeville is "a stage entertainment especially popular in theaters in the early decades of the twentieth century that consisted of various unrelated acts following one another in succession and that might include performing animals, acrobats, comedians, dancers, singers or magicians." In Fort Worth, the Majestic Theater defined vaudeville.

Built in 1910 at the corner of 10th Street and Commerce, the Majestic Theater was called one of the most beautiful playhouses in the South. The first floor lounge was decorated with love seats, mahogany chairs and a fireplace with brass andirons. In the auditorium, the Majestic had upholstered seats "soft enough to bring out the Rip Van Winkle in anyone" and a red upholstered rail in back for the comfort of standees. Ticket prices ranged from ten cents in the gallery to one dollar for boxes.

Many of the greats of the entertainment world played at the Majestic. Will Rogers, immortalized in bronze in front of Fort Worth's Will Rogers Complex, twirled a lasso and told jokes from the Majestic stage. In 1914, Mae West starred in "In A Style All Her Own." A newspaper critic at the time wrote that Fort Worth audiences were still too unsophisticated for West's broad brand of comedy. The same year, the Four Marx Brothers were a big hit in a skit called "Home Again." Sweetie Ladd painted Groucho Marx, who ended his more than fifty-year career in theater with his own television show, in the center of the lobby with his signature cigar and mustache.

Jack Benny, Eddie Cantor, dancer Fred Astaire and his sister Adele (before he danced with Fort Worth's Ginger Rogers), Eddie Foy and the Seven Little Foys, Houdini the magician, Fred Allen, the dance team of Eduardo and Elisa Cansino (parents of actress Rita Hayworth)—all appeared at the Majestic. In addition to the players on the stage, there was a full orchestra conducted by Phil Epstein or George Orum, who later became part of Fort Worth history as a conductor of the Stock Show Band.

In 1929, just prior to the Depression, Bob Hope, the Ritz Brothers, George Burns and Gracie Allen, and Edgar Bergen and his dummy, Charlie McCarthy, played the Majestic.

Eventually, the bill at the Majestic changed from straight vaudeville to vaudeville plus silent movies. In 1930, the Majestic lengthened vaudeville performances from approximately forty-five minutes to an hour and a half as a cost-saving measure because the theater was not making expenses. In 1932, vaudeville died on the Texas circuit, and the Majestic switched to motion pictures. It continued, showing primarily second-run double-feature movies, until March 25, 1953. The building was demolished in 1966.

37

The Stag Saloon at the corner of Sixth and Main streets was a favorite stop for the male citizens of Fort Worth. Sweetie Ladd painted the interior of the saloon from a 1912 photograph in the collection of the Fort Worth Public Library. She probably viewed the saloon as a little girl and was curious about what went on inside the building, but as a "properly brought up" child from a "substantial" family, she never would have been inside.

The two men behind the bar are believed to be the proprietor, W.A. Hornbeak, and Tony Porter. The decor is typical of the best saloons at the time. Among the more than three dozen saloons in Fort Worth in the early 1900s, the Stag and the White Elephant, on Main Street between Second and Third, were considered the most "upscale." The White Elephant had a solid mahogany filigree bar forty feet long, a mirrored back bar which was the "pride and joy" of the place, cut glass chandeliers, and a wide, carpeted stairway to the second floor where a table stood "stacked six inches high with gold coins." The saloon became known as one of the best drinking and gambling establishments "in any town." It has gone down in Fort Worth history—and legend—as the site of the Luke Short/T. I. "Long Hair Jim" Courtright shoot-out, reenacted each year in the Stockyards National Historic District.

The Stag Saloon boasted not only such traditional touches as a brass rail and spittoons but also electric lights and ceiling fans. It was heated by the black wood or coal stove complete with stove pipe at the right of the painting. Open both day and night, The Stag offered a menu that included oysters, fresh fish, game, dozens of meats and vegetables. Although the Stag and the White Elephant were called saloons, both were gathering places for the leading men in Fort Worth and enjoyed impeccable reputations. An early operator of the Stag, Joseph C. Wheat, grew so prosperous he was able to purchase Fort Worth's first "skyscraper," a six-story building at Eighth and Main which became known as the Wheat Building.

A far less elegant Fort Worth saloon, the Headlight Bar, advertised in the *Fort Worth Democrat* in 1876 for customers to "Ride right in, boys, and get bar service from the saddle" which may qualify the bar as the first drive-through establishment in history.

Gambling flourished in Fort Worth until 1907 when County Attorney Jeff McLean, a crusader against open gambling, was murdered by one William Tomlinson. Tomlinson fled through the Stag but died in a shoot-out with police. Members of the Texas Legislature were in Fort Worth for the Fat Stock Show at the time. Shocked, they returned to Austin and immediately passed a law against gambling. Saloons continued to operate in Fort Worth until Texas ratified the eighteenth amendment that provided total prohibition on February 28, 1918.

Some of Sweetie Ladd's most vivid memories of growing up in Fort Worth involved Sunday school picnics and what members of her generation referred to as "Kodak parties." George Eastman perfected the Kodak box camera in 1888, and in the early 1900s young people, fascinated with the simplified method of photography, not only used the cameras to record their activities but planned activities for the purpose of making pictures.

When the dam on the West Fork of the Trinity River was completed in 1914, some high spots in the terrain became islands. Goat Island, one of those high spots, immediately became a favorite recreation site. This painting, one of the few oils in the collection (Mrs. Ladd discovered that she was allergic to oil paints), reflects activity in 1915. Young people have brought tent, chairs, picnic table, and fishing poles by boat to spend a day on Goat Island. They share the island with a herd of goats either marooned by rising waters or transported to the island to control vegetation.

Parks were a major concern in Fort Worth as early as 1892 when City Park—now known as Trinity Park—was created. It was the only park in Fort Worth for many years. In 1907, Sam Davidson, commissioner of public grounds, streets and alleys, appealed to the Fort Worth Federation of Women's Club to help improve City Park. Mrs. John W. Swayne, president of the federation, and a committee of members raised $550 to pay for a gate at the park entrance.

In June the following year, Mrs. Swayne called a meeting of men and women to organize a Park League and establish a series of parks in Fort Worth. Noted landscape architect George E. Kessler prepared a park plan that was the guide for the development of the Fort Worth Park system until the 1990s. In 1909, a provision for establishment, government and maintenance of a Fort Worth park system was incorporated into the new city charter. The city purchased the part of what is now the Botanic Garden in 1912, including Rock Springs, which provided water for Native Americans, Major Ripley Arnold's dragoons, and Fort Worth pioneers. Forest Park, the city's first municipal swimming pool, opened in 1921; the first municipal golf course, Worth Hills, in 1923.

Lake Worth is still a recreation spot, but the Fort Worth Park and Recreation Department razed sagging docks and other facilities on Goat Island. The island still is owned by the city and may be rented for parties or camping.

41

The Liberty Bell was paraded down Main Street, in front of the historic Knights of Pythias Building, during a one-hour stopover on its nation-wide tour from Philadelphia. Although the bell was two hours and forty five minutes late arriving on its special train, more than 75,000 people packed Main Street from the Texas & Pacific Railroad Reservation to the Tarrant County Courthouse while the bell, on its special car, was slowly drawn past over streetcar tracks.

According to the *Fort Worth Star-Telegram*, "residential Fort Worth was deserted for three hours and the business district suddenly became a confusion of red, white and blue. Every window was alive with heads and shoulders, and the crowd spread even to the roofs of the tallest office buildings. Main Street, closed to traffic for the parade, was enveloped in flags and bunting, and men and women and children wore tiny bells and flags and waved larger flags.

"The bell was switched from the Katy (railroad) tracks to the streetcar (tracks) on East Front Street near the car barn. Some of the Philadelphia council party boarded the bell's special car and made the tour down Main Street and back, and others rode in autos with Fort Worth officials.

"Mrs. Mary Skidmore, daughter of a Continental soldier who heard the bell proclaim liberty July 8, 1776, boarded the bell car and occupied a seat of honor in front of the car. She waved her handkerchief delightedly at the cheers that rolled from one end of Main Street to the other."

After its allotted hour in Fort Worth, the Liberty Bell was taken to Arlington, where a five-minute stop was scheduled.

The Knights of Pythias Castle/Lodge Hall at 313 Main Street, completed in 1881, is now one of the architectural treasures of Sundance Square. The building was the first Knights of Pythias Castle in the world and the only one personally dedicated by the founder of the order, Justis H. Rathbone. After a fire in 1901, the building was rebuilt according to the design of Fort Worth architects Sanguinet & Staats. The knight in a suit of armor, in a niche in the building's façade, has become as much a Fort Worth icon as Molly, the longhorn on the Livestock Exchange building.

In the early 1900s, the Knights of Pythias had a statewide membership of 30,000. It was one of the many fraternal organizations that played a major role in the social and business life of American communities. In addition to Recorded Texas Historic Landmark and National Register of Historic Places markers, the building has a plaque noting that on the site from 1947 to 1952, Staley T. McBrayer and the McBrayer Publishing Company conducted research adapting the offset press to newspaper reproduction, a development which revolutionized newspaper reproduction worldwide.

Liberty Bell on a
Nationwide Tour 1915.

Sweetie Ladd '76

Sweetie Ladd remembered January 18, 1930, when the temperature in Fort Worth officially sank to nine degrees and Lake Worth froze over. Near zero was not a record low. The Fort Worth Weather Bureau recorded a low of eight and a half degrees below zero on February 12, 1899, but that was before Lake Worth was created. In 1914, when Fort Worth built a dam on the West Fork of the Trinity River to provide a reliable source of water, the lake quickly became equally important as a recreational site. Residents boasted that Lake Worth, with a shoreline of approximately forty miles, was the largest outlying city park in Texas. The lake is some twenty miles long and two miles wide, with a depth of sixty feet at its deepest point. It originally provided an estimated thirteen billion gallons of water but silting has reduced its capacity. The demands of a growing Fort Worth population required the addition of Bridgeport Lake in 1932 and Eagle Mountain Lake in 1934. Several other lakes have since been created to control floods and conserve water.

When Lake Worth froze in 1930, it provided a surface for skating and sledding in a young city that had no ice rinks. Sleds were created from wood platforms equipped with tractor seats or ordinary chairs. Children slid across the ice in their school shoes and adventuresome adults drove Model A Fords onto the frozen surface. Lake Worth froze a second time in 1949.

Although a frozen lake is a rarity, snow has been a common winter occurrence in Fort Worth. Records show a total of 15.3 inches in the winter of 1963-1964 and 13.5 inches in 1923-1924. Longtime Fort Worth residents spoke of "Stock Show weather" because the worst winter storms customarily struck in late January and early February at the time of the annual Southwestern Exposition and Livestock Show.

Some weather observers credit the system of lakes in the Fort Worth vicinity with the change in the city's climate. A 1991 Business Resource Notebook described Fort Worth's climate as "humid and sub-tropical with hot summers." The same source did concede that the area has a wide range of annual temperature extremes. Old-timers say that a "blue norther" blowing in from the plains can drop temperatures as much as forty degrees in sixty minutes. While actual winter temperatures are milder than those in much of the United States, winds which accompany Fort Worth cold snaps usually contribute a "bone chilling" effect. The U. S. Weather Bureau's reports of the wind-chill factor in recent years has produced a more accurate picture of winter weather in Fort Worth.

A rare occasion — Lake Worth Frozen

Sweetie Ladd

Fort Worth's Nine Mile Bridge was not a bridge nine miles long; it was a bridge across Lake Worth constructed exactly nine miles from the Tarrant County Courthouse. The first bridge by that name was a narrow wooden structure built in 1912 on Nine Mile Road. That first bridge became one of the original "thrill experiences" for Fort Worth drivers and caused extensive traffic jams when Sunday drivers lined up to take their turns crossing it.

By 1928 it was apparent that a new bridge was needed, and city and county officials agreed to move the new structure to the Jacksboro Highway, approximately a thousand feet northwest of the original bridge. In that position, the bridge was to have been immediately northwest of the Casino Park dance hall. Specifications for the new Jacksboro Highway bridge, built at an estimated cost of $350,000, called for a structure fifty feet wide, concrete banisters for the protection of motorists, a thirty-six-foot roadway, and seven-foot sidewalks on each side.

The new span opened May 5, 1930. A new Casino Park opened almost simultaneously. The new dance pavilion was so important to Fort Worth that the management broadcast dance programs on the radio. Fort Worth's senior residents recall dancing to the music of Glenn Miller, Wayne King, and Spike Jones under the Casino's revolving mirrored ball.

Casino Park appealed to all ages. It offered not only a bathhouse for swimmers but also a boat rental concession. There was a merry-go-round, a Ferris wheel, and Thriller—as the rollercoaster was called. Patrons strolled on a wide boardwalk past a crazy house, a shooting gallery and other concessions testing tossing and throwing skills. Casino Park burned in the summer of 1929 but was rebuilt at a cost of $250,000.

The Casino remained one of Fort Worth's most popular entertainment centers until World War II when the Big Bands that regularly played for dances were decimated by enlistments and draft requisitions. Casino Park eventually was leased but competition from more sophisticated amusement and water parks was too much, and dancers preferred air-conditioned ballrooms to the open-air pavilion. Park structures were razed, and what remained of the rides was hauled away.

When the new Nine Mile Bridge opened on Jacksboro Highway, the old bridge was kept open so it could be used "as a one-way thoroughfare to relieve congestion during big days at the Casino." Concrete piers of the old bridge remained until 1953 when members of the 949th Ordnance Battalion of the 49th Armored Division, Texas National Guard, used a $1 million army tank tractor to clear the lake for speedboat racing. Two large piers were left for building a judges' platform in the middle of the lake.

Ft. Worth's 9 Mile Bridge 1920
Sweetie Ladd '76

47

Sweetie Ladd's painting of the first home of Mrs. Baird's Bread undoubtedly was inspired by Budd Brigg's painting of the home at 512 Hemphill where Mrs. Ninnie Baird baked her first loaves of bread for sale. When Mrs. Baird's Bakeries were sold to Grupo Industrial Bimbo, a giant Mexican company, in 1998, the ninety-year-old Baird Bakeries was the largest family-owned baking company in the United States with annual sales totaling $307 million.

But in 1908, Mrs. Baird was a young woman with eight children and a husband in failing health. She started baking in her small four-burner wood-fired kitchen range. Her older sons delivered the freshly baked bread after school. At first, the Baird boys walked to make their deliveries. Later, when customers became more numerous, they made deliveries by bicycle.

When demand for her bread grew, Mrs. Baird moved her baking to a small, one-room house behind her home and installed a commercial oven that baked forty loaves at a time. She paid the Metropolitan Hotel $75 for the oven—$25 in cash and the rest "traded out" in bread and rolls. Dewey helped his mother with baking, and his brothers took over the deliveries. The four Baird daughters assumed the housework so their mother could devote full time to baking.

As production in the bakery grew, the boys' after-school delivery system had difficulty keeping up. William Allen Baird, Mrs. Baird's husband, turned the family buggy into a delivery wagon by putting a wood-paneled body on the buggy chassis. The family's horses, Ned and Nellie, pulled the wagon, and thirteen-year-old Hoyt Baird became the driver.

In 1910, the Baird family moved to a house on the corner of Cactus and Jefferson. A small house in the rear was remodeled as a bakery with a brick peel oven. The Baird boys sawed cords of wood to fit the firebox. Hoyt Baird later recalled that his mother often would accompany him on his delivery route, checking his paperback ledger of sales to charge customers. It was the only accounting the growing firm kept. If the family had money left over at the end of the month, they figured they had made a profit.

William A. Baird died in 1911. Mrs. Baird persuaded her landlord to build a wooden bakery building next door to the family's home. This building not only had a large brick oven but room up front for a retail store. Each morning, Mrs. Baird and her son, Dewey, baked bread and cakes. In the afternoon, Mrs. Baird put on a clean dress and worked in the store. The bakery did a thriving business. Cars often lined up for blocks at 5:00 P.M. while drivers waited for bread just out of the oven.

In 1919, the Baird family built its first bakery at Sixth Avenue and Terrell, bought a second delivery truck, and established a second sales route. From 1919 to 1928, the bakery was enlarged nine times. The family persuaded Mrs. Baird to quit working in the bakery in 1920, but she continued as active head of the business until her death in 1961 at the age of 92.

A Ft Worth Institution
Mrs. Baird's Bread

The Benton House at 1730 Sixth Avenue endures as Fort Worth's most picturesque Victorian cottage a hundred years after it was erected by Kansas City builder William Azro Benton for his son, Meredith Azro Benton, and the younger Benton's wife, Ella Belle Benton. The story-and-a-half Queen Anne-style residence on a corner lot is still surrounded by a replica of its original fence and still owned by descendants of the builder. The house is built of cypress, and the gingerbread trim is believed to be hand-sawn rather than machine cut. The back of the house has a lattice-screened porch that once housed a cistern to collect rainwater.

Architectural historians point out that the Benton House has all the hallmarks of a Victorian Queen Anne cottage—an asymmetrical plan, hipped roof with cross gables, spindlework, patterned wood shingles and a cutaway bay window. The interior includes fireplaces with oak mantels and doors with transoms and copper and bronze hardware, all original and carefully preserved by the family.

Meredith A. Benton, 1861-1941, was a tobacco distributor who began his career selling tobacco in Indian Territory, now the state of Oklahoma. When the house was built, it was on the open prairie and family records tell of Ella Belle Benton watching her husband's horse and buggy leave the old Texas & Pacific station on his way home from a business trip.

Sweetie Ladd rarely painted historic buildings without including people engaged in activities typical of the era, but it is obvious that some of her favorite subjects were children. In her painting of the Benton House, children are particularly appropriate because Ella Belle Benton helped establish the public school kindergarten program in Fort Worth. She also was instrumental in founding the Fort Worth Rose Society.

The organ grinder and his monkey were part of the street scene in almost every American city in the early 1900s, providing entertainment for children at a time when there was no television, no radio and no phonographs or tape players.

The Benton House is listed in the National Register of Historic Places and was designated a Recorded Texas Historic Landmark in 1981. It is part of the Fairmount/Southside National Register Historic District and the City of Fort Worth Historic and Cultural Sub-district, both designated in 1990.

Organ Grinder
Benton Home on 6th Ave
Ft. Worth, Texas 1915

51

Sweetie Ladd once told a reporter that her painting of the Livestock Exchange was one of her favorites. Her father, Edgar Kerr, was a rancher and cattleman and was affiliated with the Cassidy Southwestern Commission Company, one of the forty-two commission companies at one time housed in the Livestock Exchange. The artist remembered scenes such as that shown in the painting, with the horse-drawn Armour & Co. wagon mingling with "newfangled" automobiles and cowboys on horseback.

The Livestock Exchange was built at 131 East Exchange Avenue by the Fort Worth Stockyards Company in 1903. In addition to the livestock commission companies, the Stockyards Company, the Livestock Commission, prominent cattle, horse, mule, hog and sheep buyers, the Western Union, Livestock Marketing Association and the Southwestern Cattle Raisers Association had offices there. Every animal sold in the Fort Worth Stockyards was processed through the Livestock Exchange. Acres of livestock pens surrounded the building when it opened.

With its red tile roof, curving "Alamo" parapets, octagonal cupolas and one-story arcade, the stucco-covered brick building is considered a classic example of Mission Revival architecture, although the identity of the architect has been lost. Molly, the cast-metal Longhorn centered in the main parapet, has become a Fort Worth icon. The building was designated a Recorded Texas Historic Landmark in 1968.

By the 1970s, both the Armour and Swift plants in the Stockyards district closed, and interest rose in preservation and tourism to provide a stable economic base for the area. The building was renovated in 1977-1978 under the direction of Thomas E. Woodward and Associates, Architects.

Holt Hickman purchased the building in 1994 as part of his plan to redevelop the stockyards area as an entertainment and tourist area. The Livestock Exchange building continues to provide office space for businesses and professionals, and The North Fort Worth Historical Society, founded in 1975, has offices and a museum there. The two structures form an architectural anchor for the Fort Worth Stockyards National Historic District, which was listed in the National Register of Historic Places in 1976.

Sharing frontage on Exchange Avenue with the Livestock Exchange is the Cowtown Coliseum. The first Fat Stock Show was held in 1886 under a stand of trees in the stockyards area. By 1902, stock show promoters sought funding for a hall that would be the permanent home for the show to be called the National Feeders and Breeders Show. The coliseum, with a 12,000-seat arena, opened March 11, 1908. It hosted the National Feeders' and Breeders' Show from 1908 until 1917, and the Southwestern Exposition and Fat Stock Show from 1918 until 1942 when the event moved to Will Rogers Coliseum. The world's first indoor rodeo was held in 1918 in the Cowtown Coliseum (sometimes called the North Side Coliseum).

Enrico Caruso, Elvis Presley, Bob Wills, Roy Acuff, Harry James and his orchestra, and Diaghileff's Ballet Russe all performed at the coliseum, and evangelist Billy Sunday invited sinners to "hit the sawdust trail" in revivals held there from November 1918 to January 1919. The City of Fort Worth purchased the coliseum in 1936 and restored the building in 1985-1986 under the direction of restoration architect Ward Bogard.

Parades always have been a part of Fort Worth. The city's first "real" parade in 1878 celebrated the Fort Worth opening of the eastern terminus of the world's longest stagecoach line—the 1,500-mile line from Fort Worth to Yuma, Arizona. The Stock Show, which began in 1896 with a few animals shown under the trees on the bank of Marine Creek, had become the annual Fat Stock Show by 1907. To this day a downtown parade opens the show each January. It is possibly the longest parade in the world without motorized vehicles.

Sweetie Ladd drew the Stock Show Parade as it passed in front of the Flatiron Building at 1000 Houston Street. Built in 1907, the Flatiron Building is one of fourteen "skyscrapers" built between 1907 and 1930 surviving in the central business district. The Flatiron Building is recognized not only as the earliest remaining skyscraper in Fort Worth but also as the only true flatiron building in Texas and an important example of high-rise design outside of metropolitan centers on the East Coast and in Chicago. The seven-story building was designed by Fort Worth architects Sanguinet and Staats and constructed by the firm of Buchanan and Gilder for $70,893. The building has been saved by several owners who respected its historical significance and by the unique triangular lot on which it stands.

Dr. Bacon Saunders, a surgeon and dean of the Fort Worth Medical College, purchased the lot in 1906 and is said to have decided on the unusual architecture of the building after seeing the Flatiron Building in New York City. Originally the Fort Worth Flatiron was designed with ten stories, but it was trimmed to seven stories when the city suffered a recession in 1907. Dr. Saunders had his medical offices and laboratory on the top floor of the building, served by an elevator with an ornate iron cage. The ground floor originally was occupied by a drugstore, and many of the tenants were physicians and surgeons.

One of the most significant aspects of the building's exterior is a band above the second floor punctuated at intervals with carved panther heads. Fort Worth has been known as "Panther City" since 1876 when a Dallas newspaper described the town as so sleepy that a panther could sleep in its streets. The panther motif also has been utilized in the decor of Will Rogers Coliseum and the United States Post Office.

The Flatiron Building is listed in the National Register of Historic Places and has been designated a Recorded Texas Historic Landmark and a City of Fort Worth Landmark. At the instigation of the building's owner, Dr. George Cravens, the Flatiron has been designated a highly significant endangered building by the city.

There is an interesting personal connection between Sweetie Ladd and the Flatiron Building. For forty years, Mrs. Ladd taught the Rae Reimers Bible Class, a non-denominational Bible class sponsored by Mrs. C. D. Reimers, the daughter of Dr. Bacon Saunders. Mrs. Ladd gave up her teaching assignment to concentrate on art.

Flat Iron Building
(1907)
Stock Show Parade

55

If Nat Washer had followed his first inclination when he stepped into a large mud puddle in the middle of Main Street, Sweetie Ladd might not have had a Washer Brothers store to paint. Nat Washer's brother, Jacob, moved to Fort Worth in 1882 and rented a store between Fourth and Fifth streets on Houston. He sold ten-gallon hats, boots and bandanas, but the rent was more than the business warranted. Jacob joined Leopold August, and the firm of Washer & August thrived in the town of 6,000 people until 1867, when August joined his own brother to form A. and L. Clothing Store. Jacob Washer persuaded his brother to join him, but when Nat Washer arrived in Fort Worth in a driving rain and immediately stepped into a mud puddle, he informed Jacob that "one year at most would give me my fill of both Fort Worth and Texas."

The sun came out, the puddle dried up, and Washer Brothers became one of the major retail stores in Fort Worth. It progressed from ranch attire to tailored suits although its merchandise always included Stetson hats. The famous Shady Oak hats that *Fort Worth Star-Telegram* publisher Amon G. Carter presented to celebrities originally came from Washer Brothers although they later were supplied by Peters Brothers, a Fort Worth hat shop. When Will Rogers stayed at the Fort Worth Club in July 1935, a month before his fatal plane crash in Alaska, he bought a new shirt and blue suit at Washer Brothers and left the clothes he arrived in at the Fort Worth Club. Eventually, the store added an equally prestigious department of women's fashions and was noted for its exclusive lines of women's hats.

Washer Brothers was one of the retail establishments that made downtown Fort Worth an important shopping center in the decade following World War II. Locally owned department stores—Meacham's, Monnig's, Washer Brothers, R. E. Cox, Leonard Brothers and The Fair—competed with J.C. Penney, F.W. Woolworth and Kress for shoppers' dollars. In addition, Fakes, Ellison's and the Ladd Furniture Company offered furniture and carpets to Fort Worth residents and West Texans. By 1990, these stores had closed or moved to the suburbs.

The "black funerals" in the painting's title refers to the custom of renting black hearses for funeral processions. Family and friends of the deceased were expected to ride in all-black buggies. If the funeral were for a child, the horse-drawn hearse was white.

Livery stables were a meeting place for the whole town in early Fort Worth. Rigs were rented for $4 a day, $6 on Sunday. Dudes looking for the "surrey with the fringe on top" could choose between brightly-painted red or green buggies. Some of the best customers were traveling salesmen who came to Fort Worth on trains, then rented a horse and buggy to call on the trade for miles around. George L. Gause opened the Missouri Wagon Yard in 1876. Renting hearses became such a large part of his business that he studied embalming and opened an undertaking parlor with Frank Flenner in 1879.

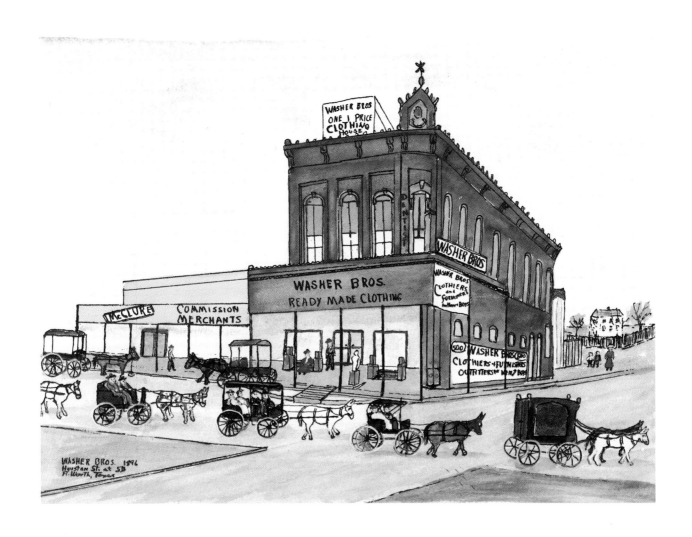

WASHER BROS. 1896
Houston St. at 5th
Ft. Worth, Texas

57

Fort Worth National Bank celebrated its centennial in 1973, and Sweetie Ladd probably was inspired by the occasion to paint this view of the bank's first quarters on the ground floor of a two-story building at 109 West Weatherford Street.

Founded as a private bank in 1873 by two former Confederate soldiers, Thomas A. Tidball and John B. Wilson, the bank was re-named Tidball, Van Zandt and Company, Bankers, a year later when Major K.M. Van Zandt, Major J. J. Jarvis and John Peter Smith purchased an interest. Van Zandt, a Confederate veteran who came to Fort Worth in 1865, was named president.

By 1880, the bank had outgrown its first quarters in the old store building and moved into a brick building at the northwest corner of Main and First streets. By then, Fort Worth's population had grown to 6,663—an increase of more than 6,000 people in four years. The private bank obtained a national banking charter on February 28, 1884, and became Fort Worth National Bank with Van Zandt as president, a position he held until his death in 1930.

Perry R. Bass emphasized the bank's role in Fort Worth's growth in his 1973 introduction of Lewis H. Bond, chief executive officer of Fort Worth National, at the Texas Dinner of the Newcomen Society in North America. "During the depression, after the discovery of the East Texas oil field, the late Sid W. Richardson owed the Fort Worth National Bank $350,000. Uncle Sid [Perry Bass is the nephew of the late Mr. Richardson] had an income of about $25,000 a month at that time. A year later, his income was down to where he no longer could pay the interest on the remaining part of his indebtedness.

"Ellison Harding, who had succeeded Major Van Zandt as president of the bank, said: 'Sid, keep what little income you're getting to live on and pay on your loan when you can.' Ellison Harding carried Uncle Sid, not only on his loan but on his office rent, for three years." In 1935, Sid Richardson and his nephew, Perry Bass, brought in the first well in the Keystone field in West Texas where oil reserves were estimated at $800 million. The resulting Richardson fortune founded the Sid W. Richardson Foundation which benefits universities, hospitals, the arts and other worthy causes.

In 1969, in the largest downtown real estate transaction in Fort Worth history, Fort Worth National acquired more than four blocks for a thirty-seven-floor glass-sheathed tower occupying a block bounded by Throckmorton, Taylor, Fourth and Fifth streets, and an adjacent five-story parking garage and motor bank. Fort Worth National moved into its glass tower in 1974. In 1982, when the name of the bank was changed to Texas American Bank/Fort Worth, its parent holding company, Texas American Bancshares, Inc., was the sixth largest banking organization in the state. Texas American Bank was among nine of the ten largest banks in Texas forced out of business by drastically declining oil prices in 1989. The bank was absorbed by Bank One in 1992.

Ft. Worth National Bank
(1873)

Sweetie Ladd
'75

In 1960, Sweetie Ladd began painting Fort Worth places and events of the early 1900s. Her first paintings were inspired by Wheatley's "Cries of London," a series of etchings of eighteenth-century English peddlers. She called the series "Cries of Fort Worth."

These paintings recall a time when tradesmen came to the housewife. This was a time of trust. Before the invention of the electric refrigerator, housewives left the back door unlocked so the ice man could come into the kitchen and fill the icebox with the block of ice weighing precisely fifty, seventy-five or 100 pounds. The size needed was indicated on a card displayed in the kitchen window.

Until the 1940s, Fort Worth grocers called their customers on the telephone each morning to get a list of required groceries. The groceries were delivered later in the day, and if the housewife happened to be away from home, the grocer placed any perishable items in the icebox. At the end of each month, when the grocer presented his bill and was paid, he usually gave each customer a can of peaches or a couple of candy bars.

When peaches and plums or watermelons were ripe or vegetables ready for the table, farmers loaded their harvests in wagons and brought them to front gates. Farmers knew when housewives made jelly, which families preferred mustard greens to turnip greens or sweet potatoes to Irish potatoes, and they made their rounds accordingly.

When Mrs. Baird began baking bread for sale, the loaves were delivered to kitchen doors in a horse-drawn wagon driven by her sons. Milk in glass bottles was placed at the front door each morning. This was before pasteurization, so the milk separated with the cream rising to the top. When temperatures dropped below freezing, milk froze in the bottles, pushing the cardboard stoppers up on a cone of frozen cream. The milk wagon had rubber tires, and milk-wagon horses were fitted with hard rubber shoes so the milkman wouldn't disturb the neighborhood when he made his rounds early in the morning. Housewives washed the empty milk bottles and placed them by the door, to be picked up by the milkman and refilled.

By the 1900s, Fort Worth's growing population and summer droughts had depleted the natural water supply. Before the construction of the city's waterworks, water carts peddled water for twelve-and-a-half cents a barrel. Water was delivered to homes and placed in a cistern from which homeowners dipped it up bucket by bucket for drinking, washing and cooking. Rainwater, prized because it was "soft" and lathered easily for washing clothes and hair, was carefully collected.

Ice cream was not an everyday treat in the early 1900s. Iceboxes could not preserve ice cream. Children eagerly awaited the arrival of the ice-cream man who pushed a cart, in the days before the more familiar ice cream truck with its characteristic bell.

There were no pizzas, no fast foods, no hamburger havens in the early 1900s. Fort Worth families cherished the hot tamale man who customarily stood in front of the laundry with his cart. The corn-shuck - wrapped tamales usually were tied with cotton string in bunches of a half dozen. If housewives were particularly busy, tamales might be served on newspaper-covered kitchen tables, accompanied by crackers and large glasses of water. When the meal was over, empty shucks were rolled up in the newspapers and discarded. People old

Vegetables

enough to remember those tamales insist they were the best Tex-Mex food ever.

In that era before radio and television news, Fort Worth residents were alerted to major news events by extras—newspapers printed with breaking news and hawked by newsboys who stopped traffic with cries of "Extra! Extra!" Newspapers received their news through leased wire services that sent stories to Teletype machines. The machines typed out stories, line by line, and alerted editors to major events by sudden silence followed by four or five loud bells. The *Fort Worth Star-Telegram* printed one of its last extra editions on November 22, 1963, when President John F. Kennedy was assassinated in Dallas.

Conservation and recycling are not exclusively customs of the late twentieth century. Pins and needles were expensive and cherished in the early 1990s but were not stocked in local stores. Housewives purchased those items from a woman called "Dearie" who brought them to homes in cases. Most clothing was made at home, and housewives and older daughters were expected to sew. Families that could afford it hired a seamstress who took up residence in the home for a week or two each season to make clothing for the family.

Knives and scissors were sharpened when they became dull, not discarded. A professional knives-and-scissors sharpener made rounds every few months. Garments worn to rags were collected by a rags-and-bottles man who went from house to house gathering scraps of cloth too stained or worn to be made into quilt tops and bottles which couldn't be refilled.

Like the newsboy, most of these tradesmen called out in a loud voice to announce their services. Thus the name, "Cries of Fort Worth."

Pins and Needles

Ice-Cream Man

Extra-Extra

65

Knives–Scissors Sharpened

Bread Man

Water Man

Ice Man

Hot Tamales

of *Rud...*
...u Reindeer.
You can catch them i...
Hysterical Blindness unti...
5 at Circle Theatre.

Bestseller: Everyone kno...
Cissy Stewart chronicled the
...ves of Cowtown's social set for
...ears. Shoot. I've been writing
...his column for almost 10 years,
...nd I *still* get mail addressed to
...issy!

Now she is **Cissy Stewart
...ale,** and she is still writing
...bout Fort Worth. Her latest
...ome, *Sweetie Ladd's Historic
...ort Worth,* published by TCU
...ress, sells for a hefty $39.95 and
...s No. 2 on the local nonfiction
...estseller list.

For those who don't know her,
...weetie was a much-loved
...owtown character who took up
...rt at the age of 60 and captured
...ort Worth from the turn of the
...entury to the 1940s with a series
...f "folk art" paintings that is
...harming. Cissy supplies an
...nformative commentary for the
...ook.

For all of us who can't know
...oo much about Fort Worth, it's a
...ust-have volume. Cissy's
...riends are snapping it up five
...ooks at a time.

Mary Rogers covers the social scene.
(817) 390-7745
rog@star-telegra...com

Rags and Bottles

This book began with a telephone call from Ginger Head Gearheart of Imagination Celebration who asked if I would be interested in writing the text for a book on the Sweetie Ladd paintings owned by the Fort Worth Public Library. A series of meetings with Linda Allmand, then director of Fort Worth Public Library, and with a potential publisher established two facts: the merit of such a book and the inability of the library to raise publication funds during a $4 million fund drive by Fort Worth Library Foundation for expansion and renovation of the Central Library building.

The expertise of Dr. Judy Alter, director of the Texas Christian University Press, and the generosity of individuals, foundations and organizations, made publication of this book possible. Major contributions were made by the Summerlee Foundation of Dallas, Kay Dickson Farman, the Fort Worth Public Library, and Friends of the Fort Worth Public Library.

Anyone who writes about Fort Worth or Tarrant County history is indebted to dozens of individuals and organizations that have preserved the area's history. Donors who recognized its contribution to local history and purchased the works from Mrs. Ladd's estate saved the Sweetie Ladd collection for the Fort Worth Public Library.

I am particularly grateful for the assistance of Ken Hopkins (manager), Max Hill (assistant manager), Shirley Apley (senior librarian) and Tom Kellam (librarian) of the genealogy/local history unit of the Fort Worth Public Library. Thanks go also to the Special Collections Division, University of Texas at Arlington Libraries, with its *Star-Telegram* and *Fort Worth Press* files, and to the library of the Amon Carter Museum. Ron Hall, who organized a retrospective of Sweetie Ladd's work for his Hall Galleries in 1986, and Vida Hughes, manager of the Hall Galleries, provided extensive information on the artist including gallery notes prepared for the exhibit by Dr. Paula Eyrich Tyler.

Donald P. Dow, Betty Dow and Gregory Dow of the Dow Art Galleries, who appraised the collection for the library, were of great help. Dr. Frances Edward Abernethy of Stephen F. Austin State University, an authority on early Texas games, was of assistance, as was Dr. John Richardson, who shared his personal recollections of Mrs. Ladd. Kathy Dolan, library development officer, was invaluable in helping arrange the difficult process of reproducing these valuable original works. I thank Judy Alter for adroit application of pressure when deadlines passed and my husband, Max S. Lale. Any errors are entirely my own.

Cissy Stewart Lale
Fort Worth, Texas 1999

Maurine M. Callahan
Mrs. Ed P. Williams
Garvey Foundation
John W. Freese
Dr. Sim Hulsey
Mrs. Adams Shugart
Nettie Griffin
Helen V. Atkins
Mrs. Joseph C. Terrell
Mrs. Irvin W. Jarrell Jr.
Mrs. Ross E. Garrett
Mrs. A. Kennedy Randolph
Mrs. Gustave E. Cranz Jr.
Mrs. Ralph E. Scott
Mrs. Reed Sass
Mrs. William B. Thompson
Mrs. John R. Thompson
Mrs. Edward M. Muse
John J. Burgess
Mrs. W. W. McKinney
Mrs. John V. Roach II
Jenkins Garrett

Mrs. Philip K. Thomas
Mrs. W. W. Collins
Mrs. Hugh Benton
Mrs. P. D. Henry
Mrs. Terrell Small
Electra M. Carlin
Mrs. Chalmers Hutchison
Susan B. Kneten
Bill Zigrang
Woman's Wednesday Club
Walsh Foundation
Tarrant County Historical Society
Virginia Richardson
Margaret J. Lowdon
Nell Oden Jackson
Mrs. Ernest Elbert
Mildred Irish
Mary L. Doebbling
Rosemary M. Rimby
Marcelle H. Hull
Rae Reimers Bible Class
NationsBank

Francis Edward Abernethy, ed. *Texas Toys and Games*. Denton: University of North Texas Press, 1989.

Judy Alter. *Thistle Hill, The History and the House*. Fort Worth: TCU Press, 1986.

Michael W. Berry. Thistle Hill Furnishings Plan. National Trust for Historic Preservation, 1986.

Economic Development Report, Department of Planning and Growth Management Services, City of Fort Worth.

Irvin Farman. *The Fort Worth Club, A Centennial Story*. Fort Worth, Texas: The Fort Worth Club, 1985.

Jerry Flemons. *Amon, The Texan Who Played Cowboy for America*. Lubbock: Texas Tech University Press, 1998.

_____, Reed Sass, et al. *The Fort Worth National Bank, Century One: 1873-1973*. Fort Worth: Fort Worth National Bank, 1973.

Fort Worth Parks & Community Services Department, Interview.

Fort Worth Public Library, organizational history, provided by library.

Fort Worth Star-Telegram, various issues.

Julia Kathryn Garrett. *Fort Worth: A Frontier Triumph*. Austin: Encino Press, 1972; Fort Worth: TCU Press, 1996.

Joseph M. Grant. *The Great Texas Banking Crash*. Austin: University of Texas Press, 1996.

Sue Greenleaf. *The Future Metropolis of Texas*. Fort Worth: H. B. Chamberlain, 1893.

Ben Gunn. *The Timetables of History*. New York: Simon & Schuster, Inc., 1979.

Joe Kirby, Fort Worth Masonic Lodge #148. Telephone interview, December 9, 1998.

Oliver Knight. *Fort Worth: Outpost on the Trinity*. Norman, Oklahoma: University of Oklahoma Press, 1953; Fort Worth: TCU Press, 1990.

Mary Daggett Lake papers, Fort Worth Public Library.

Wallace R. Lale. "Remember When the Trolley Ran Straight out to Benson Park?" *Shawnee* (Oklahoma) *Sun*, November 26, 1998.

Local Climatological Data, U. S. Department of Commerce, Fort Worth Weather Bureau.

The Mrs. Baird's Story, undated corporation publication.

Marion Day Mullins. *A History of The Woman's Club of Fort Worth, 1923-1973*. Fort Worth, Texas: Evans Press, 1973.

New Handbook of Texas. Austin: Texas State Historical Association, 1996.

J'Nell Pate. *North of the River*. Fort Worth: TCU Press, 1994.

Roze McCoy Porter. *Thistle Hill, The Cattle Baron's Legacy*. Fort Worth: Branch-Smith, 1980.

Carol Roark. *Fort Worth's Legendary Landmarks*. With photographs by Byrd Williams. Fort Worth: TCU Press, 1995.

Leonard Sanders and Ron C. Tyler. *How Fort Worth Became the Texasmost City*. Fort Worth: The Amon Carter Museum, 1973; TCU Press, 1986.

Ruby Schmidt, editor. *Fort Worth & Tarrant County, A Historical Guide*. Fort Worth: TCU Press, 1984.

Otha C. Spencer. *Staley McBrayer and the Offset Newspaper Revolution*. Commerce: East Texas Mayo Press, 1997.

Cecilia Steinfeldt. *Art for History's Sake: The Texas Collection of the Witte Museum*. Austin: Texas State Historical Association, 1993.

Tarrant County Historic Resources Survey. Fort Worth: Historic Preservation Council for Tarrant County, 1982-1991.

"Weather Digest." Fort Worth: WBAP-TV, 1971.

Mack H. and Madeline C. Williams. *In Old Fort Worth*. Fort Worth: News-Tribune, 1975.

WPA Tarrant County Histories (in Fort Worth Public Library).